Brokenness Made Whole:
The Transformation

BEVERLY D. KOPP

3-30-12

Brokenness Made Whole:
The Transformation
Freedom Series, Volume 1
Copyright © 2011 Beverly D. Kopp

All rights reserved!
Printed in the United States of America.
This book or portions thereof may not
be reproduced in any form without prior
written permission from the author.

All scripture quotations in this book
are from the *King James Version*
or *The Amplified Bible.*

ISBN 10: 1468033212
ISBN-13: 978-1468033212

Cover Design by Joel Kornowski
White Harvest Graphics
Email:joel@whiteharvestgraphics.com
Website: www.whiteharvestgraphics.com

Book Agent: Living Word Transcripts
Email: rebecca@livingwordtranscripts.com
Website: www.livingwordtranscripts.com

Dedication

I dedicate my first book to my first-born daughter, Mariah Claire; this is for you my precious gift from God. Your journey from brokenness has inspired me to never quit. I love you- Mama!

Acknowledgments

I want to thank my Lord Jesus Christ for saving, delivering, healing, and transforming me to be the whole woman He called me to be for His glory.

I want to thank my wonderful husband, Pastor Mark Kopp, who always supports me and also our daughters and I want to thank our church family and Pastors, for this book is the fruit of God's love through them.

I want to thank my book agent Rebecca and the designer of my book cover, Joel, and all the Pastors, friends, ministers and partners whose prayer and support helped to make this book become a tool in God's hand to help restore hurting women for the glory of God!

Contents

Acknowledgments

1	New Beginnings	1
2	Restoring Wholeness To Women	11
3	From Brokenness to New Identity	21
4	Make Room For Change	29
5	Changed Into God's Image	37
6	Free From Strongholds	53
7	Free From Bulimia	61
8	How To Face Your Giants	75
9	Beyond The Great Beyond	83

About The Author

Introduction

"Brokenness Made Whole: The Transformation" is Volume 1 of the "Freedom Series." Beverly shares her personal transformation testimony and journey of brokenness made whole, and tells how God set her free from bad choices, wrong relationships with men and women, and the abuse, rejection, hurt, offense, and hopelessness of feeling that no one cared or loved her.

Beverly's testimony is a life-changing book that will encourage women desperate for change to find a new beginning, and fresh start to be restored, and transformed from hurt and a broken heart. Her testimony inspires women how to receive freedom and wholeness, and fulfill their destiny.

Beverly shares how she was totally delivered, healed and transformed from the tragic traumas of a broken heart, past mistakes and failures of alcohol, drug, sexual, and food addiction.

She shares how God totally delivered, healed, and transformed her from bulimia, mental illness, manic and severe depression, tumors, sexually transmitted diseases, and sickness, and the inability to socially function.

If you felt you were a failure due to past mistakes or a slave to disease, sickness, sin, guilt, and trauma, and lost your confidence, health, peace, and joy, this book is for you.

If you came to a place where you could not go any further, felt as if your life came to a stop, and want a new beginning, and fresh start in your life, Beverly shares how to let go of your past and step into a new beginning.

This is your season to be transformed with wholeness and receive a new identity in Christ to be the woman God called you to be.

Beverly's goal is to provide the uncompromising Word of God in order to minister life to the spirit, soul, and body of the whole woman.

As you read this book, let Jesus make you whole from brokenness. Jesus Christ is the only one who can go to the core of your heart and fix whatever needs fixing. Be transformed with the "whole" you in your spirit, soul, and body.

Today is your day to receive freedom to be the woman God called you to be. God did not make you a slave to sin, sickness, disease, abuse, and a broken heart. Learn how to rest in God's presence and His Word and be healed and whole to fulfill your destiny.

This exciting book will stir you as a woman to arise in your God given place as a wife, mother, homemaker, businesswoman, grandma, and minister. As a wife, learn how to enjoy your calling to minister to your husband. Enjoy the wholeness, freedom, and joy to sow time into your husband, children, church, workplace, and friends.

Through her ministry as a pastor, conducting women conferences, and speaking engagements, many women have received total freedom from abuse, rejection, and the shame, guilt, struggle or pain from emotional, mental, physical, marital, sexual, and financial and job trauma.

So dear woman, enjoy yourself, take time to read this book, go for a walk, and enjoy your favorite coffee; go shop and take a girlfriend to lunch. Learn to relax, have fun, and enjoy your life. Today is your day of transformation to be the whole woman God has called you to be for Him. Let this be a fresh start for change.

"Brokenness Made Whole: The Transformation" is the "base" book for the other books that will follow in this series. Each book will take one aspect of her life, such as addiction and sickness and focus on that one area.

Chapter 1
NEW BEGINNINGS

(Philippians 3:13-14) *"Brethren, I count not myself to have apprehended: but this one thing I do, forgetting those things which are behind, and reaching forth unto those things which are before. I press toward the mark for the prize of the high calling of God in Christ Jesus."*

From One Trauma to Another
To New Beginning of Healing

This is my journey of brokenness made whole! I was broken in many areas due to trauma, bad choices, and wrong relationships with men and women. This journey is with my Heavenly Father who is El Shaddai and my Lord Jesus Christ.

He is my Prince of Peace, my Shalom who leaves nothing missing and nothing broken. Daily and throughout this journey, the ministry of the Holy Spirit guides me and this is my story!

This is the season for brokenness to be made whole. I was broken and had trauma throughout my life. As you go through trauma in life, it starts to take root with trauma physically, emotionally and mentally.

Because of the trauma, I was socially retarded. I could not order in a restaurant. I could not talk for myself. I was afraid of everything. Because I was broken, I became an alcoholic and drug addict.

I was bulimic and sick for many years. I had diseases, tumors, and many sexually transmitted diseases from the lifestyle I lived. When I became born again, the Lord started working and healing, and healing, and healing, and healing, and healing me. I am so grateful. To this day, I am excited about my first love and relationship with Jesus Christ. It is fresh as it was twenty years ago.

Jesus is a two-way relationship and is like a marriage. To develop relationship with Jesus, you must do your part to surrender to His Word and the Holy Spirit, flow with His will, and plan for your life, and Jesus will respond, speak to you, and do His part!

To make a marriage work, you must walk in love and do your part. No marriage is a guarantee, but takes cooperation, especially when you have many things to do.

God Is Calling Women
To Press Toward the
High Calling in Christ

God is calling women to stand up and sit next to Christ in Heavenly places. Sit next to Him in the high places so you can see your new and true identity. Press in prayer and in His presence, so you will not give up and quit doing the things God has called you to do. Press for the prize of the high calling of God in Christ Jesus.

For you to see clearly the vision, plan, and purpose God has for your life, you must take time to daily worship Jesus and sit in His presence! John 4:24 says, *"God is a Spirit: and they that worship him must worship him in spirit and in truth."*

See yourself seated in Heavenly places with Christ Jesus. Your identity lies within Him. In Ephesians 2:6, the Bible says, *"And hath raised us up together, and made us sit together in heavenly places in Christ Jesus."*

Rise up, for He has blessed you with all spiritual blessings in Heavenly places in Christ so you can fulfill your destiny. Ephesians 1:3 says, *"Blessed be the God and Father of our Lord Jesus Christ, who hath blessed us with all spiritual blessings in heavenly places in Christ."*

Rest in His Presence
Dear Woman,
Wife, Mother, Minister

As women, we wear many hats such as woman, wife, mother, homemaker, business woman, grandma, and minister. We sow a lot of time into our husbands, children, church, workplace, and friends. The Lord knows and sees this and wants to redeem time back to us.

There is nothing more refreshing than sitting down with your favorite cup of tea or coffee, grabbing a good book, reading your Bible or just plain sitting in your favorite chair and resting in His Presence.

You must be in His presence to be revived, restored, and refreshed, and regain strength to continue to minister to those He placed around you. Psalm 16:11 says, *"You will show me the path of life, In Your presence is the fullness of joy; At Your right hand are pleasures forevermore."*

Taking time for yourself is not a selfish thing. It is an act of humility, knowing you need Him and His strength. So dear woman, take time for yourself and enjoy your life.

God Did Not Make You A Slave to Sin & Guilt

Don't believe the lie of the devil, but stand strong on God's Word and stay in His presence. You are not under the devil's feet, but the devil is under your feet. You are not a failure or slave to sin and guilt, but you are blessed exceedingly and abundantly. Believe and receive all the benefits Jesus gave you in Christ. (Psalms chapter 103)

Christ has given you dominion over all the power of the enemy and nothing by any means can hurt you when you worship Him in your home, and continue to worship Him until you are lost in God's presence.

Read and declare God's Word when you worship God and pray.

Through the power of Christ working within, you can do exceeding abundantly above all you can ask or think. Ephesians 3:20 says, *"Now unto him that is able to do exceeding abundantly above all that we ask or think, according to the power that worketh in us."*

Let Go Of the Past & Step into the New Thing God Has For You

Stop remembering the past mistakes you made. You are more than a conqueror through Christ Jesus for greater is Jesus in you than the devil in the world. Stand up and declare God's promises from His Word. Use the authority of God's Word to stand against the lies of the devil and do the works of Christ.

This is the hour for you to become a new woman in Christ. This is the season of transformation and reconciliation for God has called every woman of God to the ministry of reconciliation. In II Corinthians 5:18, the Bible says, *"And all things are of God, who hath reconciled us to himself by Jesus Christ, and hath given to us the ministry of reconciliation."*

Jesus Christ wants to make you a new person today. Let go of the old things you use to do. Let go of hanging around with the unsaved friends of the world and dependency on them for your security.

Hang around with godly Christians who are stronger in the Word than you are and they will bring you into a higher place in Christ.

Let go of your past attachments to the world's ways. Let go of the past fear, hurt, guilt, shame, pain, and struggles you had when you were overtaken by sin.

Don't focus on your past mistakes and failures anymore. It is over. Take a step into your new beginning. Get your eyes on Jesus and thank Him for He has done for you and is doing. Let go of doing things your own way.

With fresh and total surrender, give everything you are and have to Christ and tell Him, "Not my will, but yours be done! I'll say what you want me to say, dear Jesus. I'll do what you want me to do. I will go where you want me to go. Not my will, I will obey you."

You Are a New Creature In Christ & the Old Life Is Passed Away

Can you see that you are a new creature in Christ and the old things have passed away? In II Corinthians 5:17, the Bible says, *"Therefore if any man be in Christ, he is a new creature: old things are passed away; behold, all things are become new."*

A new creature in Christ will talk and act like Christ and will not dwell on his or her past sins for the blood of Jesus has washed them away and He can remember them no more.

Keep your attention focused on Jesus. Place Jesus first in your heart and life and treasure Him! Jesus is the answer to new beginnings. Jesus will restore, heal, and transform you with wholeness. Jesus is the one who will make the difference in your life.

This is Your New Day
To Let Jesus Make You
Into A Whole Woman

Whatever you say and do, keep your heart tuned to Heaven and do it unto Jesus! He is here right now to make you whole. People or things cannot restore you, but only Jesus can restore you and He is the one who will make you whole.

Dear woman, I want to tell you that Jesus cares for you! He paid the price for you so you do not have to live in sin and carry the guilt, shame, and sorrows of the world. Recognize who stands for you this day. It is Jesus and He came to make you whole. The transformation is already set in motion. Let this be a new day for you!

This is the day of your new beginning. Jesus is the beginning and the end. Doing the will of God is not always easy, but you must keep your focus on Jesus.

Season for a Fresh Start
& New Beginning In Ministry

Chapter 1- New Beginnings

Are you ready for a new beginning in your life or ministry? Did you come to a place where you could not go any further and felt like your life or ministry came to a stop?

All you need to do is to let God give you the fresh start that He wants. Let go of your old ideas, plans, agenda, and programs and He will cause you to do a new thing that you have not done before. Let the Spirit of God take control of your life and ministry and everything will change for the good.

Maybe you had a ministry and you could not continue it due to great adversity, lack of help or funds. Let God give you a new beginning to start fresh.

In March of 2005, my husband and I were called into "special needs adoption." Temporarily, the ministry of *"Dear Woman"* was put on a shelf. I said to God, "If you ever want to bring this ministry back, then that's great! If not, then that's none of my business."

Later on, the Lord was stirring me for a couple of months and spoke to my heart. He was giving me new ideas and plans for a new beginning and fresh start to do the work He called me to do. He said, *"Dear Woman Magazine."* I said, "Magazine?" He showed me a vision of His will and plan.

Keep your focus on Jesus. Clearly write your vision that God gives you. That is what we did. We made plans to work on many new things. I encourage you to do something with what God has put in your heart.

Take the first step and God will give you the second one. Take the second one and He will give you the third. Do it a step at a time and God will give you the people and means to get it going.

Only the ministry and vision that is dead to self and built on Jesus will stand. If you feel you lost what you once had, let go of the past and God will give you a fresh start.

As you seek the Lord, He will restore you with a new beginning that is more effective and stronger than before and will produce greater harvest and reach multitudes all over the world. Hook up with God's call, vision, and plan and watch the Lord give you increase of souls and it will grow.

The hand of the Lord will be upon the ministries and ministers that are sold out to God's heart for harvest and on fire for God. Isaiah 66:14 says, *"... and the hand of the LORD shall be known toward his servants, and his indignation toward his enemies."*

The hand of the Lord will be evident by His glory that will defend them with the funds and means to get the job done and they will be free from oppression and fear!

Chapter 1- New Beginnings

Chapter 2
RESTORING WHOLENESS TO WOMEN

(1 Thessalonians 5:23) *"And may the God of peace Himself sanctify you, and may your whole spirit and soul and body be preserved blamelessly at the coming of our Lord Jesus Christ."*

Season for Wholeness

In this end-time hour, God is restoring wholeness to women and using various ministries to challenge them to be all they can be for Jesus Christ.

This is the season of wholeness! God wants you whole in your spirit, soul, and body and every part of your life. It is God's will for you to be whole and prosper in all areas of your life. In III John 1:2, the Bible says, *"Beloved, I wish above all things that thou mayest prosper and be in health, even as thy soul prospereth."*

He wants you completely restored, transformed, and whole in all areas of your life. Do you need God to restore wholeness unto you? Have you lost your peace and joy of the Lord due to bankruptcy, divorce, tragedy, or death of a child, spouse, or loved one? Are you struggling with a hidden sin or offense?

Let me share with you what the Bible says about the word "whole." In Psalms 119:2, the Bible says, *"Blessed are they that keep his testimonies and that seek him with the whole heart."*

In the above scripture, the word "Blessed" means "Happy." The key to being a happy woman begins when you worship the Lord with your whole heart. This begins when you first wake up in the morning and worship Him throughout the day and before you go to bed at night.

In the previous scripture, the Hebrew word for "seek" is "darash" which means, "follow, seek or ask and worship." Seek the Lord and mean it with all of your heart.

Wholeness Comes By Worshiping God With Your Whole Heart

Let me share with you an example of desperate faith and the power of worship when you mean it with all your heart and the results bring wholeness.

In Matthew 15:22, the Bible says, *"And, behold, a woman of Canaan came out of the same coasts, and cried unto him, saying, Have mercy on me, O Lord, thou son of David; my daughter is grievously vexed with a devil."* At first, Jesus did not answer a word.

The disciples told Jesus to send her away because she was crying for help. In verse 24, Jesus said He was sent to the lost sheep of the house of Israel.

The woman persisted and did not give up and quit. She came to Jesus and worshiped Him saying, *"Lord, help me!"* In verse 26, He answered and said, *"... It is not meet to take the children's bread, and to cast it to dogs."*

In verse 27, she responded to Him with great faith and said *"... Truth, Lord: yet the dogs eat of the crumbs which fall from their masters' table."* In verse 28, he answered her and said, *"... O woman, great is thy faith: be it unto thee even as thou wilt. And her daughter was made whole from that very hour."*

In the above scripture, the word "whole" means to, "cure, heal, and make whole." Instantly, Jesus cured her daughter and made her whole. Jesus called her a woman of great faith. This is the power of worship and faith.

Wholeness is Restored
By Loving God
With All Your Heart &
Meaning It

Mean it with every part of your heart by surrendering yourself afresh unto God and do it heartily unto the Lord. That is genuine worship and pleases God when you make it a lifestyle to worship

God at home while no person is watching and you are doing it unto the Lord.

To worship God with all your heart means to love Him with everything that is within you. The blessing of the Lord will overtake you, as you love the Lord with all your heart, soul, mind, and strength.

Jesus said that all the law hangs on covenant love. Love God with your whole heart and love your neighbor as yourself. Examine your heart if you love God and really mean it or if your life is built on selfishness.

Matthew 22:37-40 reads as follows, *"Jesus said unto him, Thou shalt love the Lord thy God with all thy heart, and with all thy soul, and with all thy mind. This is the first and great commandment. And the second is like unto it, Thou shalt love thy neighbor as thyself. On these two commandments hang all the law and the prophets."*

Let's go to the story about the woman who took a step of faith to be made whole. She suffered for twelve years with a flowing blood disease. The Bible describes it as an issue of blood, which was the "hemorrhaging" of her blood.

Despite her condition, she pressed her way through the crowd and said within her heart that once she touches the hem of the garment of Jesus, she will be made whole. Matthew 9:21 says, *"For she said within herself, If I may but touch his garment, I shall be whole."*

When you touch Jesus with all your heart and take an act of faith on His Word, He will respond and make you whole. This is what the woman did. Her act of faith made her whole. Matthew 9:22 says, *"But Jesus turned him about, and when he saw her, he said, Daughter, be of good comfort; thy faith hath made thee whole. And the woman was made whole from that hour."*

Instantly, she became completely healed and whole and was never the same. God changed her entire life by the touch of faith.

Jesus wants to make you well in your body, spirit, and soul, so you will be sound and whole. The Bible says that Jesus made the man whole that had a withered hand. He told him to stretch forth his hand and suddenly, God restored it and it was whole like the other. (Matthew 12:13) In this scripture, the word "whole" means "healthy, well in body and whole."

Everyone Who Touched The Hem of His Garment Was Made Whole

When Jesus came into the land of Gennesaret, they brought unto Him all that were diseased, and every person who touched the hem of His garment was instantly made perfectly whole.

Matthew 14:35-36 says, *"And when the men of that place had knowledge of him, they sent out into all that country round about, and brought unto him all that were diseased. And besought him that they might only touch the hem of his garment: and as many as touched were made perfectly whole."*

Here in this scripture, the Hebrew word for "whole" is "diasozo" which means, "to save thoroughly, cure, preserve, rescue, heal, make perfectly whole and save."

In Mark 6:53-56, the Bible says that they ran through the whole region and began to carry the sick in beds from villages, cities and the country and they laid the sick in the streets and asked Jesus if they could touch the border of His garment.

Instantly, Jesus cured, delivered, and made whole all the sick people who touched His garment with a touch of faith. In this scripture, the Hebrew word for "whole" is "sozo" which means saved, delivered, healed, and made whole. Jesus did not only heal the people, but He made them whole.

Cast Yourself
At the Feet of Jesus
& You Will Be Whole

The Bible explains how great multitudes came who had the lame, blind, dumb, maimed and many others with them and when they cast them down at the feet of Jesus, He healed them and they were made whole.

Matthew 15:30-31 says, *"And great multitudes came unto him, having with them those that were lame, blind, dumb, maimed, and many others, and cast them down at Jesus' feet; and he healed them. Insomuch that the multitude wondered, when they saw the dumb to speak, the maimed to be whole, the lame to walk, and the blind to see: and they glorified the God of Israel."* In this scripture, the word "whole" means "healthy, well, sound, and whole."

Key to Wholeness:
Do Not Fear,
But Only Believe

In Luke 8:49-56, the Bible describes a story about the daughter of a man who had died. Jesus told the man to not fear, but *only believe* and she would be made whole. When Jesus came to the home, he brought inside with him the father and mother and Peter, James and John.

To those who did not believe and were weeping, He told them to weep not, because she was not dead, but was only sleeping. The unbelieving crowd laughed him to scorn knowing that she was dead. Jesus told them to get out of the house.

The miracle happened when those present had "only believed and did not have fear." Jesus spoke to the girl to get up. Instantly, the power of Jesus Christ raised her from the dead and completely made her whole. This is what happens when believers unite in faith, refuse to fear and only believe.

Are You Desperate To Be Whole?

In John chapter 5, verses 1 through 9, the Bible says there was a great multitude of impotent folk who were blind, halt, and withered. They were waiting for the moving of the water at the pool called Bethesda. An angel would come down at a certain season.

When an angel troubled the water, the first one in the water was totally made whole of the disease he had. Jesus had compassion for a man who had an infirmity for thirty-eight years, and laid there in that condition for a long time. He said to the man, *"Wilt thou be made whole?"*

The impotent man answered him, *"Sir, I have no man, when the water is troubled, to put me into the pool: but while I am coming, another steppeth down before me."* Then Jesus said to him, *"Rise, take up thy bed, and walk."* Immediately, the man was whole, took up his bed, and walked. Suddenly, he was healthy, sound, and whole.

When Jesus saw him in the temple, He said, *"Behold, thou art made whole: Sin no more, lest a worse thing come unto thee."* Instantly, he was whole from his previous sin and restored to perfect health in his body.

When there is a broken relationship with God, you will suffer from defeat to tragedy-to-tragedy, failure to failure, and will not be able to walk in victory until you come with desperate hunger to get back your first love for Jesus.

Come to God with fresh hunger to be changed and filled with the joy of the Lord. Pursue God's Word and presence and get so lost in Him until filled with His glorious presence and you are whole.

Chapter 2- Restoring Wholeness To Women

Chapter 3
FROM BROKENNESS TO NEW IDENTITY

(Isaiah 61:1) *"The Spirit of the Lord God is upon me, because he has anointed me to preach good tidings unto the meek of the earth: he hath sent me to bind up the brokenhearted, to proclaim liberty to the captives, and the opening of the prison to them that are bound."*

Don't Hook Up With Your Past

Your identity is not your past before you knew Jesus Christ. Your identity is not people, things, a position, reputation, name, fame, or your job. Your new identity is a new creature in Christ. Don't hook up with your past, but hook up with what the Lord is doing in this hour.

Identify with Jesus Christ and compare yourself to Him by putting His Word first place in your life. This comes through personal relationship with Jesus Christ and His light will shine bright within and cause you to see that you are a victorious woman in Him.

Brokenness Made Whole By The Holy Spirit

Chapter 3- From Brokenness to New Identity

Let me share with you about your new identity and the transformation process. This end-time move of the Holy Spirit is about "Brokenness being made whole."

This is the season for your brokenness to be made whole. In Psalms 147:3, the scripture says, *"He healeth the broken in heart, and bindeth up their wounds."* The anointing mends broken hearts and sets the captives free. The anointing will overtake you with everlasting joy. Jesus loves you and has great compassion for you!

A home cannot be a home with just a whole man. It has to have a whole woman so the children can be whole. All over the world, women are in need of healing and restoration, because they are the chief primary influence on the children of the world. Broken women produce broken children. Broken children multiply themselves into more broken children.

The Holy Spirit is moving and setting up His ministry to bring about God's divine will and purpose on earth.

In Acts 2:17-18, the scripture says, *"And it shall come to pass in the last days, saith God, I will pour out of my Spirit upon all flesh: and your sons and your daughters shall prophesy, and your young men shall see visions, and your old men shall dream dreams. And on my servants and on my handmaidens*

I will pour out in those days of my Spirit; and they shall prophesy."

Jesus Is the Only Answer
To Restore a Broken Woman
With Wholeness

Many have reached out to the needs of women through women's lib promotion or exaltation of the woman. They were trying to elevate her to equality with man and indeed, she is equal to man.

There is no way that the woman is subservient or below the man. God created men and women equal. He created them equal, but brokenness has put the woman down on a lower level.

Controlling women have tried to elevate and exalt themselves to usurp authority over men. They seek to usurp authority over men because men have oppressed them, but it has not worked! Only by submission to Jesus Christ will it work to be restored. Restoration and brokenness made whole will work when you let Jesus make you whole.

When Women Are Restored,
Homes & Governments
Will Be Restored

Throughout the world, as women allow Jesus to make them whole, change will come to homes and governments. In every sphere and realm where whole women walk, change will come that brings balance in the home.

In this hour, God will restore and make women whole. That is what He loves to do. Outside of Jesus Christ, there is no restoration, wholeness, or peace. Through Christ, He has given you restoration, wholeness, peace and all His benefits.

Hook Up With the Joy of the Lord
To Fix You & Keep You Strong

If you desire for God to fix you in any area of your life, you must hook up with the Holy Spirit. In Psalms 51:12, David said, *"Restore unto me the joy of thy salvation; and uphold me with thy free spirit."*

Jesus is a good carpenter and knows what makes you happy. I am not talking about being joyful. I am talking about being happy when your emotions are filled with the presence of God and you are actually happy.

The year of 2008 was the first time I experienced happiness in my life and presently I am experiencing daily happiness. The joy of the Lord keeps me strong. Before that time, I was grateful and thankful, but I was not happy.

I did not know that I was not happy. I was a good laugher and I still am, but there were many reasons why I was not happy. I can rejoice and praise God that I am happy today!

You Are Royalty & The King's Daughter

The Bible says that the King's daughter in the inner part of the palace is all-glorious. Psalms 45:13 says, *"The king's daughter is all glorious within: her clothing is of wrought gold."* Notice that her clothing is inwrought with gold.

I love the song that sings, "Fill that place." Jesus wants to come in and fill that place within your heart that is the inner you. He wants to fill that inner palace with gold.

Your King is Jesus and you are the King's daughter! Do not act like what you use to be before you knew Christ. Old things have passed away. You are royalty and God wants you to act like Him!

You are special and one of a kind! You are His jewel and beloved of the Lord. He wants to make you a vessel of honor unto His glory, honor, and praise. God has called you by His name and created you for His glory.

In Isaiah 43:7, the scripture says, *"Every one who is called by my name: for I have created him for MY GLORY, I have formed him; yea, I have made him."*

The Transformation Process: From Glory To Glory You Are Being Transformed Into His Image

The Spirit of God brings light. He clothes Himself in light. As you continue to look at that light as in a mirror, the glory of the Lord constantly transfigures you into His very own image in ever-increasing splendor, and from one degree of glory to another.

From the Amplified Bible, II Corinthians 3:15-18 says, *"Yes, down to this [very] day whenever Moses is read, a veil lies upon their minds and hearts. But whenever a person turns [in repentance] to the Lord, the veil is stripped off and taken away. Now the Lord is the spirit, and where the spirit of the Lord is, there is liberty, freedom, (emancipation from bondage, freedom.) And all of us, as with unveiled face, [because we] continued to behold [in the Word of God] as in a mirror the glory of the Lord, are constantly being transfigured into His very own image in ever increasing splendor and from one degree of glory to another; [for this comes] from the Lord [Who is} the Spirit."*

In Christ, you move from one place to another and that inner palace and inner you will continually get cleansed, brightened, and shined. That is how you get more and more beautiful!

What happens is that it starts to spill on the outside, and then all of a sudden, you look good! You look good and a little makeup helps! It's okay. My pastor says, "It doesn't hurt to paint the barn." That is okay.

By getting into God's Word and presence, His very own image is ever increasing splendor from one degree of glory to another, for this comes from the Lord who is the Spirit. As you behold the Word and look unto Jesus, the Holy Spirit will continue to transform you into the image of God. This is a transformation process.

I Am Not What I Was.
I Have a New Identity!

I'm not what I use to be! Do not freeze your present identity by looking at the past. My present identity is not a drug addict, alcoholic, and whore. In the book of Romans 6:7, the Bible says, *"For he that is dead is freed from sin."* That woman is dead. I do not feel anything when I talk about her. She is dead!

My life is hid in Christ and that is my identity. My affection is set on Jesus Christ. In Colossians 3:1-3, the Bible says, *'If ye then be risen with Christ, seek those things which are above, where Christ sitteth on the right hand of God. Set your affection on things above, not on things on the earth. For ye are dead, and your life is hid with Christ in God."*

I have no sentimental value to that old lifestyle. I have compassion for her because there are many women who are like what I use to be. God has been working on me for twenty-two years. I have been called by Him when I was in my mothers' womb.

Chapter 3- From Brokenness to New Identity

CHAPTER 4
MAKE ROOM FOR CHANGE

(Acts 2:2-3) *"And suddenly there came a sound from heaven as of a rushing mighty wind, and it filled all the house where they were sitting. And there appeared unto them cloven tongues like as of fire, and it sat upon each of them."*

Season to Change

God wants to make many changes within you! Don't get overwhelmed by the need to change. If you came to a standstill in your life, business, or ministry, it is time to make a change.

When you let go of the thing that was not God and change, then you will experience life and freedom like you never had before.

The Holy Spirit is life and never brings you sorrow, bondage, destruction, or death. He causes you to experience life and liberty. *"Now the Lord is that Spirit: and where the Spirit of the Lord is, there is liberty."* (II Corinthians 3:17)

When you do your part, God will do His part. You can do something about your life if you are sad, discouraged, or depressed and you live a frustrating and miserable life. Today, you can make room for change!

If you make room to be depressed and think there is no hope for your situation, then you will have a sad life. If you see by the eye of faith that all things are possible with God and believe His Word, this is how you make room for the joy of the Lord and joy is what you will get.

What You Make Room For Will Control You

Whatever you make room for in your desires, words and attitudes is what will control you. If you enjoy yielding to temper tantrums and lust and make room for it to control your words and actions, then strife and division will not leave your household unless you repent and make room for love to rule your heart.

If you make room for bitterness and will not forgive the wrong that people did against you, God will not forgive you. Mark 11:26 says, *"But if ye do not forgive, neither will your Father which is in heaven forgive your trespasses."*

If you enjoy lust and anger and make room for the works of the flesh to control you, it will bring you trouble.

Make room for change by yielding to the Holy Spirit to let the peace, love, joy, and fruit of the Spirit to rule you continually. Then you will walk in new levels of victory you never experienced before.

You cannot let the anointing control you and at the same time let the world rule you. You need to change to obey God for you cannot serve two masters.

The Bible states this in Mathew 6:24, which says, *"No man can serve two masters: for either he will hate the one, and love the other; or else he will hold to the one, and despise the other. Ye cannot serve God and mammon."*

Change by Surrendering
It All To God

Change by surrendering it all to God and go with the fresh plan and vision He gives you that brings joy, peace and liberty. Let it all go! Step into change and you will find increase of vision, souls, finances, health, and prosperity when you do what God wants you to do.

Change by Taking
The First Step

Change cannot take place unless you make the first step to change. If you want restoration, change in your character to let honesty, love, and faithfulness rule you. To see miracle results, change to speak words of faith and talk like God talks.

To walk in prosperity, change how you handle your finances and get around prosperous men and women of God who are successful and they will give you wisdom to make the necessary changes.

Change by getting into obedience with God. You do not have to know how to do all the steps, but you only need to obey and do that first step of obedience. God said to me that there are many, many changes and I need you to make room for the changes.

Pruning Comes Before Greater Blessings

When the Lord is pruning you and taking something out, there is something better for you. When He removes something out of you or takes something out of your life that was not of God, He will give something that is bigger, better and multiplied.

God will not tell you the second step until you take the first step. You must take that first step. You might ask, "How do I do that?" You must develop relationship with Jesus and trust Him to hear His voice. Ask, seek, knock, and wait until you get your answers. Pray in faith and move into the will of God.

Do You Want Change?

You must trust Him to take that first step on whatever God is directing you to do in your life.

Prepare for change for there are many changes He wants to make.

There are two different groups of people wanting change. The first group of people are those who are hurt bad enough that they do not have anything to lose. That is where I was.

Maybe you ask, "What do I have to lose?" You will have to lose your flesh and that is it. The whole walk is going to cost you your flesh!

Let go of your old patterns of thinking, your old habits, and everything that is ungodly. That is what it is going to cost you.

That is the price you pay and you will not care about the cost because you want change. The other type of people wants change, but they do not know how to get it.

Step Out of Your Comfort Zone On the Glory Road

The faith road and obedience to God is the glory road. The glory road is not the safe and comfortable road. Recently, when I was studying the Word, the Lord said, "Being comfortable is very affordable. It's very cheap. Comfort is easy! Going for the gold is a tough training ground. It's tough!"

The Holy Spirit will comfort you through change. (John chapters 14 & 16, II Corinthians 1:2-9)

You can stay safe and comfortable or you can go deeper in God and do what you have not done before. God is not going to be mad at you. I am not going to be mad at you, but there is a higher ground every time you move with God. There is more! It is endless! It is endless in the walk with Him.

You can stay safe and comfortable or you can step out on the Glory Road. As Pastors, my husband and I are going to go down this Glory Road. Some said to us, "Do you have to go through everything?" We answered, "Yes, we do!" because the easy way is simply the easy way!

The Glory road is not tradition, religion, or formulas. It is not the road of comfort or convenience, but it will cost you to deny yourself and follow the example of Jesus.

Luke 9:23-24 says, *"And he said to them all, If any man will come after me, let him deny himself, and take up his cross daily, and follow me. For whosoever will save his life shall lose it: but whosoever will lose his life for my sake, the same shall save it."*

You have seen yourself in a certain way for so long, but God wants you to do something completely new! Will you obey Him? Will you stake everything on the new vision and trust Him for the ability, the resources, and the outcome?

Yield to the Holy Ghost and as you yield to the anointing, it will break every yoke and bring liberty for where the Spirit of the Lord is, there is liberty.

Chapter 4- Make Room For Change

Chapter 5
CHANGED INTO GOD'S IMAGE

(II Corinthians 3:18) *"But we all, with open face beholding as in a glass the glory of the Lord, are changed into the same image from glory to glory, even as by the Spirit of the Lord."*

In this chapter, I will share some of my life story to encourage women who have gone through abuse and want change.

As you read this story, I pray you let the Holy Spirit change you from glory to glory into the image of God. Spirit, soul and body, you can be spiritually transformed into the image and likeness that God put in you and this is what you need to pursue.

Did You Ever Feel Like You Could Not Hold a Job or Had No Communication or Social Skills?

Recently, I remember having a vision and I said, "All my life I was retarded." I was a "retarded" person. Some people do not know that they are "retarded" or slow.

I could not hold a job. I could not communicate and I had zero social skills. My confidence was "missing." Getting sober was the first step to this area of change.

Symptoms of a Broken Spirit
Caused From Bondage, Control,
Domination & Abuse:

1. Loss of Your Will
2. Rejection: Stripped of Confidence
3. Loss of Ability to Function Normally

Bondage, control, domination, and abuse will cause you to suffer rejection, strip your confidence in God, yourself and others, and cause you to have no ability to function normally in life.

Let me share the vision I had the other day. I saw a napkin that was flat and it a symbol of me. I was like that napkin. I was flat. I asked the Lord, "What was that in that time?" He said, "You were totally stripped of confidence. You had zero functional ability. You had the inability to function."

I Was Like A Caged Animal!
I Used Alcohol to Take Away
Sadness But Grew Worse

God spoke to my husband and said, "Tell your wife that her Spirit was broken like a horse or caged animal that came from bondage, control, domination, and abuse."

The bondage, control, domination, and abuse flattened my spirit and I became "retarded" during that time. It was then when I drank and I drank and I drank and I drank and I drank and I drank and I drank. I slept with anyone who would sleep with me always looking for acceptance.

That was my lifestyle, but God changed me after I gave myself to Christ and there has been transformation! I do not identify with her anymore. I want to reach more women and tell them, "I was there. Come this way!"

I Took Drugs to Try To Take Away My Inner Hurt, But Grew Worse

During that "retardation" period, it grew worse and worse. Later, it grew worse than that and then it became worse until I was overtaken with drugs. One drug was not enough. In time, speed was not good enough, I took cocaine, and I took whatever I could get.

How Bad Do You Want Change?

I felt like I knew, "nothing about nothing." At that time, there was a woman in my life who was my counselor and said to me, "Are you ready for change? Do you want change? How bad do we want change?

My counselor said to me, "Are you ready for change?" I said, "Well, what's wrong with me?" It was within two weeks that I was at a treatment Center. I was seeing her due to depression.

I went there with the attitude, "Maybe there is something wrong with me and maybe they can find out what it is." I said, "I know I just can't function, but I'm sure they'll help me."

I had insurance and a job that covered the bill and even the toothpaste. I was excited about getting that Crest tube. I was excited that it was Crest and not the cheap brand. I had to grab onto something. It was important to me that I could use Crest.

I was twenty-six years old and went into a place that was the women's unit. We were in our women's group. They started talking and I thought, "I am with the right group, and in the right place." Day by day, I was with these women in group therapy and counseling.

Bondage, Control, Domination
& Abuse First Began After
Hanging with Bad Friends

Let me back up and tell you about my family background. I grew up with abundance. My parents were wonderful people and they well provided for my needs. In the early years, my father drank, but in 1968, he quit for his family.

Let me tell you what happened to me. One day, I realized that I had the wrong friends and went the wrong way with most friends in my life.

You will become like the friends you hang around. That is why you need to talk to your kids about their friends. Bad company ruins good morals, whether you are a teenager, a twenty year old or a seventy year old.

As a woman, you need decent women friends. Proverbs 13:20 says, *"He that walketh with wise men shall be wise: but a companion of fools shall be destroyed."*

New Beginning Transformation Process:
I Began To Realize That Alcohol, Drugs & Sexual Immorality Masked the Broken Spirit, Rejection & Loss of Confidence

I was in that treatment center and day by day, I started to feel better. I started walking again. I could see clearer. I started to realize that I was an alcoholic. Then I realized and was thinking, "I can't drink. I can't do drugs. That's what is wrong with me."

All of that masked the broken spirit, rejection and the stripping of confidence. I started to change and learned to live without alcohol and drugs. It was then when that new beginning transformation process started in my life.

It took about two years for me to feel comfortable about being sober. I remember going to a bar and ordering a diet coke. I sat there and thought, "No, this isn't for me anymore."

Let Go of Your Old Friends & Hang With New Friends

I started going to AA and NA. I changed and had all new friends. I did not hang out with the old crowd anymore and I never saw any of those people. They were no longer a part of my life. Many times, as you become transformed, people will fall off or you just walk away.

When people do mountain climbing and climb to the summit, there are many dead people still on those mountains. When you keep climbing to the summit, there are people in your life that fall off. Let them go! If they leave you, just wave them bye.

The Bible says to go after the sheep that was lost and not the one that left. Luke 15:4 says, *"What man of you, having a hundred sheep, if he lose one of them, doth not leave the ninety and nine in the wilderness, and go after that which is lost, until he find it?"* If friends leave you, let them go.

Manic-Depressive, Severe Depression & Could Not Function Socially

In that process, I was diagnosed as manic-depressive with severe depression and they said that I could not function socially. That was my diagnosis. I learned to study and believe God's Word.

Encouragement for Single Women: How I Met My Husband & Was Married

My past was not "bright" in regards to relationships, dating or men in general. In this book, I will not get into all the details regarding my past, but I will tell you the story of how I met Mark, my husband of twenty-two years.

After the treatment center released me, I was learning to live drug and alcohol free. Everything in me was starting to be unmasked. I had come out of a relationship that lasted three years and it almost destroyed me. After the treatment, I started to attend the Narcotics Anonymous meetings and met many new people.

I remember the girlfriend who was my roommate for about a year. At that time, she was a true strength to me. We went to meetings together. We cried together and she would read the Bible to me.

One day, she handed me a prayer that was a dedication to God. This prayer stated that, from this day forward, I was going to let go of all of the "old" relationships in my life and that the next man in my life was going to be the husband that God chose for me.

To this day, I remember reading that prayer, and the power it had for me at that time in my life. One month later, I was attending a Narcotics Anonymous meeting and when I looked across the room, there was a man sitting with his arms crossed.

He wore a yellow polo shirt and Levi jeans. He had a lazy eye and a silver tooth. He seemed to be alone in the midst of the sixty people in the room. At that time, that meeting was the largest in the county.

We were enjoying this new freedom of being sober and drug-free. With what I am about to tell you, I never had this happen to me before. When I looked at Mark and I heard the words, "You're going to marry him." I looked around to see if anyone else had heard these words!

Could this be the prayer from a month ago? In time, we started to talk, went to meetings together, out to lunch and then on a date. I did not pursue him, but I pursued peace. After two months of dating, we went to another Narcotics Anonymous meeting and he "dressed up" for this one. Those were most of our dates.

He wore polyester bell-bottom tan pants and a "western shirt" with snaps. Yes, snaps! Get this. Are you ready? He wore platform shoes! Normally, I would have crawled under the table, but this time I sensed a peace in my heart that I had not yet known.

It was as if his heart was open to me and I loved him. I got past the pants, the shirt, and even the shoes and I pursued the newfound peace I was first learning to sense. This man was not the "norm." He was different. I was excited and scared at the same time. Unlike the others, he was gentle and nice to me.

Most of all, he had a job! He had a sense of purpose and goals. I liked that he was not married. He had a car that was very strange because I was the girl with the car and the money in most of the old relationships.

With courtesy and respect, he opened the car door for me and still honors me like this! I remember when he first gave me a ride in his car. I was amazed because he brought me home at a decent hour.

In time, I learned that I was rooted in religion. I was a modern-day Pharisee and had been judging others from the outside. Jesus came to bring His Kingdom to us and to pierce the hearts and souls of humanity. God has given the Holy Spirit to us. He is the outpouring of the heart of our Father.

Today, I do not mix my "who" and my "do." I know who He is, who I am, and what I am called to do. My worth is in Christ. What I do is a result of that relationship.

Mark and I were married two years after that first date. He said he liked me because I was "different." So the two of us "different" people were called together into the ministry and together we produce a "different ministry."

It was different from what we both knew and different from what we both came from. Our ministry is full of different people with different callings and different backgrounds. We are blessed to be different.

So dear single woman, do not let the one get away that your Heavenly Father has for you. Be sensitive to His leading. He will arrange your marriage and your husband will be perfect for you. He will be different from what you thought.

Do not let him get away. Do not ignore him or assume he is not the one, because he is different from what you have seen in men. Jesus was different. The Pharisees were looking for someone else and missed Him. Pursue the Peace. Get past the pants. Get past that Jesus was the carpenter's son. Your Prince awaits you!

Done With Sickness & Diseases

Frequently, I was sick when I was a child. I was hospitalized for pneumonia and severe stomachaches. I was a nervous child and this contributed to the recurring stomachache problem.

I had boils on the back of my legs, which had to be lanced. I had a seven-inch tumor in my left jawbone and had six surgeries on it. In addition to that, I had a bone transplant from my hip that into my jaw bone. This was when I was eighteen years old. I was released from the hospital with a clean bill of health, when I was 24.

Along with the help from the treatment centers for drug addiction and bulimia, I now know that all my past problems had contributed to the many years of depression I suffered. The doctor diagnosed me as manic-depressive and medicated me.

After two years, I flushed those meds. Today, I continue to walk step-by-step in divine health, knowing it is my Father's will for me to be whole.

I know the devil wanted to take me out when I was a child. I am not in the past and will never identify with it. I am not there for I am a new creature in Christ. In the Amplified Bible, II Corinthians 5:17 says, *"Therefore if any person is [engrafted] in Christ (the Messiah) he is a new creature (a new creation altogether); the old [previous moral and spiritual condition] has passed away. Behold, the fresh and new has come."*

Do you know what happens when you are born again? You receive Jesus and your spirit is sealed, but you still have a soul that consists of your mind, will, and emotions.

Emotions are how you feel! As a woman, you have emotions and can feel them. You are high in emotions until you get that thing submitted to the Holy Spirit.

There is order that comes in transformation and you have a body that needs to be surrendered to God along with your emotions. Romans 12:1 says, *"I beseech you therefore, brethren, by the mercies of God, that ye present your bodies a living sacrifice, holy, acceptable unto God, which is your reasonable service."*

You Are Changed Inside Out
By Renewing Your Mind with The Word
& Being Filled with God's Presence

When you are born again or saved as the Bible calls it, your soul is not saved. You must renew your mind to have a new thinking pattern that is not conformed to the world, but to God's Word.

Romans 12:2 says, *"And be not conformed to this world: but be ye transformed by the renewing of your mind, that ye may prove what is that good, and acceptable, and perfect, will of God."*

Renew your mind through the written Word of God to get a new thinking pattern. Read and study the Word with hunger for change within and then obey.

Every time you attend church where called to attend, your mind is renewed as you listen to the

Word. Hearing the Word preached or exhorted strengthens your faith so you do not get distracted or yield to sin.

Having fellowship by exhorting one another in the Word will help to keep you strong in the faith and encouraged in the Lord. Hebrews 10:25 says, *"Not forsaking the assembling of ourselves together, as the manner of some is; but exhorting one another: and so much the more, as ye see the day approaching."* The Word of God renews your soul.

Each time you are in God's presence, the more your emotions get healed and free from the sorrows and pressures of the world and He will refill you with joy.

Let me share an example about your emotions. If you wore a certain perfume with your old boyfriend and smelled that perfume later on, you would think of him or would see or think of something and your feelings would kick in. Those are emotions! Your mind thinks about something and your will kicks in and says, "I want this." In other words, these are called "soul-tie triggers." Smells, sight, and taste can trigger an emotion.

All those areas need to be strengthened by the presence and Word of God, and come into subjection to the Spirit. After that, your body starts to change because God works from the inside out.

I Married Because I Feared
No One Would Love Me & Thought
I Would Escape From Abuse!

At the age of twenty, I married for the wrong reason. I thought that no one else would love me and knew that I was not in love with the man. At that time, I thought I needed the security of that relationship. That was the reason why I married him in 1981.

Previously, I had been in a long relationship with the boy from high school and the fear of him was overwhelming due to him being controlling and mean. I thought that if I married the man, it was a way to get away from the abusive relationship with the previous controlling boy.

I married with the hope that all the abusive comments would stop which I heard repeatedly from the boy I knew since high school. The boy would say, "You're a fat pig! You're a whore! Nobody wants you now. I don't even want you anymore. You're fat and ugly. I am going to call you Dumbo."

Through all of that, a stronghold came on me because of having sexual union with him. Girls and young women, I want to tell you that every time you have sex outside of marriage, it is illegal in God's eyes and you take on all the spirits that comes with that union. That is when a "soul tie" is formed between you and that person.

In that way, you received a stronghold that starts to form and bondage begins. The stronghold of abuse will cause your personality to change and the real you will fade away.

Due to believing a lie that there was no one else who would love me, and thinking, I would get away from the abuse. That is why I married the guy I didn't love, but the marriage only lasted for three and one-half years.

I drank almost daily and had numerous affairs. After that was over, once again, I became involved with the boy from high school. After I was sober awhile, he called me and I was able to hang up the phone. I saw him one time again and I was able to walk away.

Your Identity Is Not
Your Past

Your identity in Christ is not connected to your past sin, failures, or body image. You are not a product of genetics. You are not a product of what someone said about you. You are not a product of your parents, but you are a daughter of the King and His blood flows through you. Christ has given you all things that pertain to life and godliness.

II Peter 1:3 says, *"According as his divine power hath given unto us all things that pertain unto life and godliness, through the knowledge of him that hath called us to glory and virtue."*

Chapter 5- Changed Into God's Image

CHAPTER 6
FREE FROM STRONGHOLDS

(II Corinthians 10:5) *"Casting down imaginations, and every high thing that exalteth itself against the knowledge of God, and bringing into captivity every thought to the obedience of Christ."*

> A Stronghold Holds You
> In Bondage Due to
> Wrong Way of Thinking

God wants you from strongholds. In this chapter, I want to share with you about strongholds in the lives of people. I want to identify poverty, obesity and any kind of addiction.

A stronghold is an area in your life where you are held in bondage due to a wrong way of thinking. You can overthrow and destroy strongholds by casting down everything not of God in your thoughts and bringing every thought into submission to God's Word.

In my mind, I once believed that drinking alcoholic beverages, blacking out and passing out was normal. I remember telling my parents, "All my friends drink, and so do their parents. So, what's wrong with you?"

Chapter 6- Free From Strongholds

This kind of thinking was a stronghold that disagreed with God's Word. These triggers will affect your emotions. Also, certain perfumes will "trigger" emotion. Later in life, I pulled down the alcohol stronghold that was in my mind and saw it as a lie of the devil and I have the victory over it.

In the Amplified Bible, II Corinthians 10:4-5 says, *"For the weapons of our warfare are not physical [weapons of flesh and blood], but they are mighty before God for the overthrow and destruction of strongholds, [Inasmuch as we] refute arguments and theories and reasoning's and every proud and lofty thing that sets itself up against the [true] knowledge of God; and we lead every thought and purpose away captive into the obedience of Christ (the Messiah, the Anointed One.)"*

Walk in the Spirit &
You Will Not Gratify
The Cravings &
Desires of the Flesh

In the Amplified Bible, II Corinthians 10:3 says, *"For though we walk (live) in the flesh, we are not carrying on our warfare according to the flesh and using mere human weapons."* Now, what is flesh? The flesh is your old system of thought patterns.

To understand the flesh, turn to Galatians 5:16. From the Amplified Bible, it says, *"But I say, walk and live [habitually] in the [Holy] Spirit, [responsive to and controlled and guided by the Spirit]; then you will certainly not gratify the cravings and desires of the flesh (of human nature without God)."*

The flesh is the human nature without God. It is like peace verses arguing. We are not going to debate anymore. You do not need my opinion and I do not need yours. I want to know what God's Word says.

In verse 16, the Word "walk" means, you do not go back to your old neighborhood. Don't walk in that area. It is like someone that knows his old neighborhood. Every once in a while, he wants to drive by it for the purpose to go back and see what it is like.

The Bible says the flesh and Spirit are at war with each other. In the Amplified Bible, Galatians 5:17 says, *"For the desires of the flesh are opposed to the [Holy] Spirit, and the [desires of the] Spirit are opposed to the flesh (godless human nature), for these are antagonistic to each other [continually withstanding and in conflict with each other], so that you are not free but are prevented from doing what you desire to do."*

God's Presence Will Move Out Ungodly Desires

Do you know how to move out of the flesh and not oppose the Holy Spirit? Move out of the flesh by sitting in the presence of God and letting Him touch you. Pray, get in the Word and attend church.

In His presence, He will move out those desires that were not His character and move you into His desires as the Holy Ghost does surgery.

In God's presence, He will anesthetize you with peace or supernatural laughter, as He removes whatever is not of Him. While you are laughing, He is doing a work within. He is adjusting you. He is pruning you. He is removing all those unnecessary things of the old that prevents you from moving forward so you can produce and have results.

> If You Do The
> Works of the Flesh,
> You Will Not Inherit
> The Kingdom of God!

Let's read what the Bible defines as the works of the flesh. In the Amplified Bible, Galatians 5:19 says, *"Now the doings (practices) of the flesh are clear (obvious): they are immorality..."* This includes adultery and fornication. Sex before marriage is illegal in God's eyes. You are not protected. Trust me! You can get full of diseases. It's an open door for destruction.

There is no covenant with sex outside of marriage or adultery. It is wrong. When you first hear that, it takes time to learn that and believe that and all of a sudden, you cannot be talked out of it. That is how He works. Some call it being "old fashioned." Well, then I am "old fashioned" to His Word.

In the King James, Galatians 5:19-21 says, *"Now the works of the flesh are manifest, which are these; adultery, fornication, uncleanness, lasciviousness, idolatry, witchcraft, hatred, variance, emulations, wrath, strife, seditions, heresies, envyings, murders, drunkenness, revellings, and such like: of the which I tell you before, as I have also told you in time past, that they which do such things shall not inherit the kingdom of God."*

The works of the flesh are impurity, indecency, idolatry, sorcery, witchcraft, enmity, strife, and jealousy. You do not have to be jealous of anyone. That is a trap of the enemy. You are valuable and unique to God.

Concerning the comparison trap with women, their body image, jealousy and all that junk, it absolutely will not get you anywhere. It is a delay. Comparing yourself with other women is a distraction and it is not fair to you or her. You are unique and there is only one of you!

You are special! God says you were fearfully and wonderfully made. In Psalms 139:14, the Bible says, *"I will praise thee; for I am fearfully and wonderfully made: marvelous are thy works; and that my soul knoweth right well."*

Alcoholism, Drug Addiction & Bad Temper Is Sin & Not a Disease

Selfishness, bad temper, divisions, party spirit, envy, and drunkenness are sin. These are not diseases. They are sin. It is a generational spirit. My husband and I came together and said, "Alcoholism, drug addiction and divorce stops with us. It will not affect our children."

Our adopted daughter received a name change and took on us! She looks like my husband. Her physical and spiritual genetics changed. All of it changes when adopted into our family.

Through the adoption process, God is showing us what He does and what it takes to get someone born again, again. She gets born again, again and then born again. She gets born again in the natural. She gets a new name. She gets a new birth certificate and then she will be born again by His Spirit That is what happens to us.

We are called by a new name. We have a new blood line. We need to study and understand these things and we can do these things. By faith, you have to take your stand to reach those dreams God put in your heart. That is what I did.

With confidence I said, "I can reach those dreams. We can go places. I am not going to sit here, be stuck, and never reach those dreams that are in my heart."

The other day, a lady came to us weeping. She was fired from her job of twenty years. She said, "God's been dealing with me for two years to leave my job." I said, "Well, if you don't leave your job, He will make sure you will leave one way or another. Being fired is one way. I have seen this happen more than twice."

Then I asked her, "What's in your heart that you want to do?" She said, "I hated that job. I wanted to be a nutritionist. I've already got 4 years of school." I said, "Go follow your heart. Your heart is where God lives."

I Was the Prodigal Daughter

My story is the prodigal daughter. I grew up in church and with provision. I left all that, for what? I was deceived. I left it all behind, served the devil, walked in the mud, and played with the best of them in the dirt.

The prodigal daughter is my story. I believed that was right, even though in my heart I knew it was wrong. You can be so far gone in some things or you get comfortable in a certain lifestyle and that is all you know.

I watched soap operas since I was a little girl. I watched them for twenty years and I thought that was normal. I lived soap operas. Now, I cannot stomach a soap opera. It is full of adultery and lying.

God Wants To Give You A New Identity

It is God's purpose to give you a new identity. He wants to transform you. Receive a new transformation through the blood of Jesus that wipes all things not of God in your heart and life. You are joint heirs with Christ. You have an inheritance and are transformed through Christ, the Anointed One and His Anointing!

Chapter 7
FREE FROM BULIMIA

(2 Corinthians 10:4-6) *"For the weapons of our warfare are not carnal, but mighty through God to the pulling down of strongholds; Casting down imaginations, and every high thing that exalteth itself against the knowledge of God, and bringing into captivity every thought to the obedience of Christ. And having in a readiness to revenge all disobedience, when your obedience is fulfilled."*

Through careful strategies, Satan sets up cunning deceits. He sets up a "stronghold" in one's mind. Let me give you an example. Regarding obesity, the first time you overeat, that is when that stronghold starts. If you do not give in to it, then that thing is not going to grow.

The Holy Spirit Will Show You Things to Come

Every family has "familiar" spirits. I always slice that word and it is *"fami/liar."* There are assignments from the enemy to destroy your family. If he cannot get grandma and grandpa, he will go to the next generation, the next one, and the next one.

You never know if he is going to hit. The Bible says the Holy Ghost will tell you of the things to come and warn you of the approaching enemy.

This scripture made me want to know the Holy Ghost. John 16:13 says, *"Howbeit when he, the Spirit of truth, is come, he will guide you into all truth: for he shall not speak of himself; but whatsoever he shall hear, that shall he speak: and he will show you things to come."*

Here is the process of that set-up. This is what he does. First, it is established in the mind, which is your thinking process. Behind this fortress is a lie.

The devil says, "Don't you really need that food? Don't you feel better now that you overate? Don't you feel comfortable?" This is how Satan talks.

Take Authority Over Wrong Thinking

When the devil speaks, he will say, "Nobody is going to know. Who's going to find out if you have an affair?"

I remember when I was at a gas station one day. Someone gave me one extra dollar of change. I ran back and returned that dollar. At that time, I knew it was not right to steal.

The Word Works

When I went to treatment, I was at a 7th-9th grade level and I was twenty-six years old. My mind was tired; it needed to be full of the Word.

I was saved about a year. Then, I went to Nursing Assistant School for six weeks and graduated at the top of my class. I was thirty years old, just married, saved, and going through school and was the top of my class. I have been doing CNA work since 1990 and the Lord trained me. He worked with me.

What It Took To Get Me Free

After being saved, I set aside the first five years and all I did was study the Word. I listened to tapes night and day; I studied the Word. That is all I did. I went to church every Wednesday and Sunday. I went to prayer. I went to conferences. I did anything I could to get free. That is what it took.

Change What You Can About Yourself & Let God Transform Your Heart!

If you identify with the past or failures, you will be stuck with that old image. God wants you to see His image of who you are in Christ. If you want to lose weight, you will have to change in your food and exercise habits. Learn to listen to the Holy Spirit regarding your body.

One day, the Lord spoke to me and said, "I want you to start working out at the gym with a personal trainer." I thought, "huh?" I was a great athlete and worked out a lot, but I had not done aerobics for fourteen years. Within the last three years, I did not do one leg lift or abdominal exercise.

I went to the gym where He told me to go and hired a personal trainer. On that first day when I was ready to go, she said, "This is what we're going to do first." I said, "I can't do that!"

She said, "I want you to do three sets of that right now!" I thought, "Am I paying you to yell at me?" I was not going to argue with her. She is a professional body builder and I was out of shape and "no sculpt." I had a one-pack, which I could not find. You are supposed to have a six-pack and I could not even find my one-pack.

I started working out on a specific program. I had been going seven weeks and He said, "Five times a week." I went there five days a week and worked out ten hours a week. I said, "Lord, I'm not ready." but that was where I was at that time.

My identity was what I weighed. I am not talking about, "I am what I weigh." That is bondage. I came to the point when I said, "My whole family is obese. They are all 300 pounders. I'm just going to accept this. I don't have the energy."

I did not have the energy, but part of that was what we went through with our daughter and the adoption. There was some stress in our lives. The Lord knows if there has been stress in your life. Is so, you need to do a sit-up or two to relieve that stress. You need to walk and do whatever it takes.

I was with a personal trainer. She weighed and measured me and took my BMI and I was just "ugh." Do you know what happened during that time? The Lord was ministering to me and He said, "You're going to be that woman that you see and you're not going to identify anymore with being a product of genetics. You may look like your family, but you are not the product of genetics!"

The blood of Jesus overrides genetics! You are not the product of what someone else said about you! The blood of Jesus overrides those words and you are not a product of your parents! My identity was changing.

You are the product of Jesus Christ and are victorious for He has given you the ability to walk in health and be strong in your spirit, soul, and body. Jesus has given you the ability to be the woman God has called you to be for His glory.

Bulimic For 9 Years

The second treatment center I went to, was because I was bulimic for nine years. I vomited because I was so tired of being overweight. I would throw up. I took laxatives and water pills and said, "I wanted to change. I needed the treatment center."

They said my heart was getting weaker, my throat was burned from the vomit, and I said, "I need change." I had insurance! For four weeks, I went to the treatment center for bulimia and never threw up again. I learned some things about myself. Also, I learned how much control there is in food. (I will have more on this in another volume.)

I Lost Weight
By Eating a Little of
Whatever I Wanted

Not one time, did I overeat for seven weeks. God did that and I dropped twenty pounds in seven weeks. Today I eat whatever I want and whenever I want. If you put the law on yourself by thinking, "You can't eat ice cream, and you can't have cake," you are going to fail! You are free when you get to that place in God that you can eat whatever you want.

If I want some ice cream, I will have it, but I will eat a half cup and enjoy it. I will not throw up and feel guilty or nag my husband because I ate ice cream. It is done. The old me is dead!

If I want pizza, I will not eat the whole thing at 10:00 at night. I will have a piece or two. God did it. Do you know what He did? When I started preaching on strongholds, that was when the change came in my life.

All my life I tried dieting. It did not work. The first time in my life I was not on a diet, I did not overeat and worked out five days a week.

Today, I am not on a diet. I do not eat what you eat. You do not eat what I eat, and I am not supposed to weigh what you weigh. We do not have the same workout because I am not you, and you are not me.

Jesus Made You Free From The Desire for Alcohol

Behind every fortress, there is a lie. The devil says, "You are going to stay drunk." The Word says, "You can do all things through Christ who strengthens you!" Stand on God's Word as your strength.

Say what Philippians 4:13 says. You need to say, *"I can do all things through Christ which strengtheneth me."* Through Christ, you are already free from that bondage. You are not going to stay drunk for Christ has already made you free from alcohol.

Jesus Made You Free From Poverty

The devil says you are going to stay poor. Know your benefits in Christ. Poverty and lack does not belong to you. II Corinthians 8:9 says, *"For ye know the grace of our Lord Jesus Christ, that, though he was rich, yet for your sakes he became poor, that ye through his poverty might be rich."*

You are not going to stay poor as you stand on God's Word and give to the poor. When you give to the poor, you will be blessed. Proverbs 22:9 says, *"He that hath a bountiful eye shall be blessed; for he giveth of his bread to the poor."*

As you give to the poor, God will cause you to not lack. Proverbs 28:27 says, *"He that giveth unto the poor shall not lack: but he that hideth his eyes shall have many a curse."*

Jesus Made You Free From Overeating & Bulimia

The devil says you are going to stay overweight, but Christ says you are not going to stay overweight and unhappy about yourself. You need to say, *"I have overcome bulimia and see myself victorious from being overweight because John 4, verse 4 says that greater is Jesus in me, than the devil that is in the world."*

Jesus Made You Free From Deceit & Dishonesty

The devil says you are going to stay a liar. You need to take authority over that lie by speaking what the Word says. You need to say the following.

"Devil, the Bible says in John 8:44 that the devil was a murderer from the beginning, and abode not in the truth, because there is no truth in him. When you speak a lie, you speak about yourself, for you are a liar and the father of lies. The truth lives in me and in John 8:32, the Word says that the truth has made me free from all lies."

Jesus made you free from the bondage of dishonesty and deceit. You are not going to stay a liar. Surrender yourself to God's Word and see who you are in Christ.

You are victorious over all the lies of the devil. You are a godly woman of truth and righteousness. Romans 6:18 says, *"Being then made free from sin, ye became the servants of righteousness."*

Jesus Made You Free From Stealing or Coveting Your Neighbor's Spouse, Car, or Things

The devil says you are going to stay a thief and steal from others. In Christ, the sin of covetousness no longer belongs to you. Christ has made you free from coveting your neighbor's spouse, car, and material goods.

See your benefits in Christ. God has blessed you with benefits. Psalms 68:19 says, *"Blessed be the Lord, who daily loadeth us with benefits. Selah."*

You are not a slave to robbery. You have already overcome the sin of stealing and no longer does it have power over you to make you a slave to it.

Remind the devil what the Bible says. Tell him that the devil is a liar and the father of lies and God is true and has made you free from lies. The devil is the accuser of the brethren who had accused the saints before God day and night. (Rev. 12:10)

Resist the devil and he will flee from you. You are not going to stay a thief. Remind the devil that you are in Christ and you are not going to be a failure in everything you do.

When the devil reminds you of your past failure, remind Him of his defeat and that Jesus already defeated him and caused you to triumph over him and you are more than a conqueror through Christ who loved you. Romans 8:37 says, *"Nay, in all these things we are more than conquerors through him that loved us."*

Jesus Made You Free From Guilt!!!

If you dwell on your past mistakes, this is guilt and will keep you carrying your sorrows and prevent you from your healing and victory in Christ.

When the devil reminds you of past mistakes, sin, shame and guilt, tell him the following. "Jesus blotted out all my guilt from past mistakes and shame. I will not remember them anymore because Jesus does not remember them. Jesus has blotted them out and God remembers my sin and past no more." In Isaiah 43:25, the scripture says, *"I, even I, am he that blotteth out thy transgressions for mine own sake, and will not remember thy sins."*

Jesus Made You Free From Anger & Temper Tantrums

You are not going to be a yeller. You are not going to be unkind. See who you are in Christ. You are more than a conqueror. You are not defeated.

You are not going to be mentally ill and drugged up for the rest of your life. Make up your mind and believe it with all your heart and you will not be mentally ill or drugged.

If you will apply this to your life, you will be free! What God did for me, He will do for you. He delivered, healed, and transformed me and He will do it for you. After doing all the sinful things I did in the past, God saved and changed me. What He did with me, He will do for you and set you free too!

Maybe you don't have half the problems that I had, but you can be free from any problem that has kept you bound and hindered your ability to function as the woman of God He called you to be for Him. Apply this truth and you will be free from any bondage in your life.

Step Out of Your Personal Prison into Freedom

A stronghold is your personal prison. It is like living in a jail. It is a place of personal bondage where God's Word has been subjected to an unscriptural or personally confused idea that is held to be true in your life.

A stronghold sets your mind to believe, say, and expect something contrary to faith in God's Word. You are inviting disease, and premature death to come on your body, if you believe and say, "All my relatives died of high blood pressure or heart attack, and so will I." Those spirits will accommodate you when you give them room in your thoughts, words, and life.

When You Are Transformed, Your Words & Passion Change

When you turn into a lady, your mouth changes and not every other word is "F" this and "F" that. No longer will you talk the devil's language. No longer will you say, "You're an idiot! You're stupid and so am I and you're a jerk and moron." A new creature in Christ does not talk the devil's filth and dirt language anymore.

A transformed woman will speak wholesome words of love, joy, peace, patience, faith, gentleness, goodness, and self-control that brings live and not death to herself and others.

Woman of God, see yourself changed and know that God changed you. You have depth and meaning with your life. In Christ, you are royalty and of great value and He has made you a vessel of honor unto God.

II Timothy 2:21-22 says, *"If a man therefore purge himself from these, he shall be a vessel unto honor, sanctified, and meet for the master's use, and prepared unto every good work. Flee also youthful lusts: but follow righteousness, faith, charity, peace, with them that call on the Lord out of a pure heart."*

As a transformed new creature, you have passion in your life and it is not lust. It is passion for the things of God. That passion spills over into loving yourself and then you can love others.

As He pours His love within, you can love yourself. Then that love will pour out into society and you will change your world as a whole woman. God has called a transformed woman to change the world around you!

Behind The Lie Is Fear

It is a lie if one thinks he or she is traditionally or religiously true. A lie holds one in bondage to a formatted truth. God has made you free from religious traditions of men and the systems of this world.

There is a lie behind the lie what you always believed. I was told a lie that said, "On Sundays, if I don't go to the church that you grew up with your whole family for 150 years, you will die and go to hell."

That was not true. You go to church because you want fellowship with born again Christians and you need each other, more than ever. Behind the lie is fear. Going to church does not set you a ticket to Heaven.

Behind the fear is an idol. Food, poverty, and addiction idols are established wherever there exists a failure to trust. Jesus Christ, the Holy Ghost, and Father God are your comforters. Trust in the provisions of God through Jesus.

Chapter 8

HOW TO FACE YOUR GIANTS

(II Timothy 1:7) *"For God has not given us the spirit of fear, but of power and of love and of a sound mind."*

BE BOLD!!

Every woman of God must boldly face her giants and not be afraid. Like David, you must run at that giant with God's Word.

The thing about a stronghold is that fear is a joke! It is very real, but it is not true. There is no truth in a lie. There is no truth in fear.

There is no truth in control. There is no truth that you are fat, ugly, stupid, and dumb. Those words are lies. If you hang around the wrong crowd, you will start hearing some of that and you have to get out of there. You need good and godly friends. That is when it is fun.

Spiritual Weapons That Pull Down Strongholds

Do you know how to pull down a stronghold? You can cast down a stronghold by declaring God's Word, the blood of Jesus and the name of Jesus.

The Bible tells you to be a hearer of the Word and not only a hearer, but a doer. James 1:22 says, *"But be ye doers of the word, and not hearers only, deceiving your own selves."*

Obey God to do what He is personally telling you to do. Be a doer of the Word. Daily, you have to do the Word. Do it little by little and step-by-step. Year after year, you are changed and transformed from glory to glory.

Use your authority in Christ by applying those spiritual weapons of your warfare. Use the name of Jesus, Word of God and blood of Jesus to pull down a stronghold and confront the bondage and it will be broken.

Concerning my testimony, I have shared that I was bulimic. I shared when I was at treatment. I shared when I was at the gym. I had to confront all of those "big deals" in my life. I have to and continually have to face everything!

When I stood on the scale, I could not believe what I weighed. I did not go the place I use to go, because I could not find it anymore, but I sensed that place of shame and fear was gone. I spoke aloud what I weighed and I said, "You couldn't have even said that before. It's a number. Okay, so you've got to lose some weight. It's time God's dealing with you. Whenever, you are ready. It's time and you are enjoying it. It's going to be great. It's going to take me about a year to get to where I want to be and find my 'second' pack. If I ever have a six-pack, I will send out letters."

Previously, I threw up for nine years, drank alcohol for about twelve years, overate since I was eight years old, and exercised vigorously.

It was not going to take three days to drop the poundage. He does not work with me that way, but day by day, a balanced pace.

My story is that I had to go the long route because throughout this whole process, character was being developed. I am not spoiled.

You cannot even convince me to drink. Do you see the difference? There is a change. God gives you strength when you surrender it all to Him.

Until this point, my story is my whole life. God is doing a new thing in us and He is a God of strength. Isaiah 40:29 says, *"He giveth power to the faint, and to them that have no might he increaseth strength."* He wants to give you everything He has, but you have to receive it and move out of the way.

You will never be able to convince me to go back to the bars. Those familiar spirits are gone.

Remember that the enemy is perverted and he is not a creator. He will bring half-truths.

He is a deceiver and liar and wants you to start believing the lies. When the Holy Ghost comes, He has a still small voice, is a gentleman, and speaks truth.

Did I have to go through treatment to the gym? No, I did not have to go through treatment, but it was presented as a means to help me.

I fit in my home, church and the ministry God gave me! I found my place and I am going to keep it. I am not giving anything away. I am keeping my place and going for it and our church members are going to do it together.

A stronghold is a long-term problem. It says, "I can't overcome and I've done my best." I asked the Lord why it was easier for me to keep off the weight at that time. He said that I had masked the stronghold by excessive exercise and that was how I was bulimic.

Sometimes, I daily worked out for four hours. Therefore, I kept off the weight by quieting down the stronghold by the exercise, but never dealt with the stronghold. I believe that many people do that.

Presently, God is dealing with me on my need for balance concerning food choices, portion size, and health. I cannot work out four hours a day or even for one hour a day, nor do I want to do it; balance is the key in all areas.

Various Ways
To Identify Strongholds

Let me give a couple of ways to identify strongholds. There are emotional, mental, speech, sex, addictions, infirmities, and religious error strongholds. You can identify a stronghold in another area if there are symptoms. For example, a stronghold says, "I can't do it."

Do you have a long-term problem? Do you go back and forth your whole life with that problem? It may be like the weight. It might be up, down, up and then down. The weight really shot up and I could not move, as I desired to move. I like production. I like to exercise. I like to work. I had to start thinking about that and I could not move as I once use to move. I was tired.

To Face Your Giants,
Get A Strong Word Foundation &
Be Faithful To Your Church

Some say, "You mean I have to go to church every week?" I answered, "Yeah! You don't have to, but you get to go." There is a mindset right there. Some say, "I have to go to work." Thank God, you have legs and that you can go. Get a new attitude. I have said, "You got night sweats and gambling debts, but if you get a new attitude, that's going to change."

From the prophetic signs happening every day, it seems Jesus is soon to return. It is urgent for each member of the Body of Christ to find his or her place and remain faithful so we can all be productive in God's plan and Kingdom!

The local church is the hub from which all ministry gifts are to function and the center out of which they are to flow. In the local church, you can find what is needed to build the charter of Jesus Christ in you.

Each member of the Body of Christ, the church, is a living organism and not an organization. You should discover your gift and calling as you connect to the local church that God has designed and placed you.

Submission is vital for your success. You are in submission when you get under the mission or vision of the Pastor of the church where God has placed you. The local church is a family designed by God.

The Pastor is the spiritual father of that Body and his wife is the spiritual mother of that Body. You are part of the family for that Body that Christ has put together. All are being adopted into that family.

People will come from different backgrounds, religions, ethnicity, and other cities. As you join your church family, you are one in the Spirit where there is unity.

UNDERSTAND 4 ASPECTS OF THE LOCAL CHURCH

1. A Church Is A Place of Love!!!

Church is a place where the abused, rejected, fatigued, and hurting can come to find believers, who understand, forgive, love, and accept them. They need a place of safety, refuge, and protection.

2. A Church Is Based on The Word of God!!!

Jesus is the Head of the church. He has placed local Pastors as His under-shepherds. He has designed the church in a special order so that He may give commands or direct them through His Word and His Spirit to reach His people.

A Word Church is a local church that establishes the Bible as its doctrines and regulations, rather than the traditions of men.

3. A Church Is A Teaching & Training Center

Teaching gives you instruction and training provides hands on experience. You need both to be successful at what you are given to do.

4. A Church Is An Outreach Center

The church is called to reach people for Jesus and has been commissioned to go into all the world and preach the Gospel to every creature. (Matthew 28:19-20) By training believers, the church will be equipped to go into the community.

The church are those called-out ones, the remnant of God and those born again, who consist of His Body. The body of Christ come together to edify, encourage and comfort each other. The body come together to hear from the Lord and King who has saved them!

We come together to be refreshed, loved, forgiven and accepted. When you meet together with praise and worship, the Lord is exalted as King. You and I are the church and God needs you to do your part and fulfill His call to win souls to Jesus.

You must be bold and fearless to face your giants. Within your thoughts, you must cast down every stronghold that does not agree with God's Word. Use God's Word, the blood of Jesus and the name of Jesus. Resist the devil and he will flee from you.

The devil is a liar. Jesus has given you power and authority over all devils and nothing by any means will hurt you, as you trust in His Word, name and the blood of Jesus.

Chapter 9
BEYOND THE GREAT BEYOND

(Colossians 3:1) *"If ye then be risen with Christ, seek those things which are above, where Christ sitteth on the right hand of God. Set your affection on things above, not on things on the earth. For ye are dead, and your life is hid with Christ in God."*

My Prayer for You

Agree with me
As I pray for you today!!

"Father God, I thank you for answering the questions of the woman reading this book. I thank you for correction. I thank you for giving direction to every woman reading this book.

Father God, I thank you that fear goes in Jesus name. In Jesus name, I take authority over all the spirit of fear in your life. I speak to fear right now. In Jesus name, fear, you are recognized and exposed so this woman and daughter of the King can reach her God given potential and destiny.

God, I thank you that she is not going to linger another forty years, but is going to reach her destiny. I thank you for every assignment and ministry made clear to the woman reading this book. I thank you for that in the name of Jesus.

Father God, I thank you for going to the roots and taking her beyond the beyond. She has crossed to the other side and is going forward. Holy Spirit, I thank you for encouraging her. I thank you for that.

I thank you that you are her comforter, advocate, stand by and strengthener. Thank you for your ministry and the demonstration of the Holy Ghost and power.

I thank you Lord that the impossible becomes possible through the yoke-destroying anointing that works within the woman of God reading this book.

I thank you for this day and hour when women rise in ministry by God's glory and power of Christ. For Pastors who read this book, I thank you that they are going to rise to a new level, receive strength within them and listen to God's Word as you minister to them.

I thank you for every woman, mother, grandma, and aunt reading this book. Thank you Jesus for what you are doing. Thank you for readers to have eyes to see and ears to hear your voice. I praise you for it and thank you Lord. In Jesus name Amen."

Let God Take You
To New Places in Him

God wants to take you to new places in Him. He is going to break soul ties. A soul tie will keep you bound and familiar to a woman, man, job, or old house.

Some say, "I wish I had my house back. I miss my house." Do you know how I would respond to that comment? I would tell them to move into the new house. It is that simple.

A woman once said, "I want my old car. I love that car." She was asked what happened to that house. Her answer was, "It fell apart." The greatest need is emotional healing. It is a feeling. You get hooked on a feeling and you are hooked.

Last week, my husband fired me and said, "You're fired. I am done with you. You are always waiting for that emotional feeling. Why do you always need a feeling?" He fired me. Well, he has fired me before and he hired me back. I was glad. He said, "You're the only woman I know that needs a staff of seventy people."

Moses is dead and so are the car and the house. God wants to meet you at the depths of fear, not the surface of feelings, or your behaviors. Some are trying to modify behaviors and it is not working. Move in trust and let Him intervene.

Let God Take You Beyond Circumstances, Logic & Control

He wants to take you beyond circumstances, logic, and control. Women are good controllers. At one time, I did not like women. I never liked women. I was afraid of women. I said I would never be a lesbian.

Spiritually, I was almost in cardiac arrest when God said, "You are going to minister to women." I fought it, and I fought it and fought it even more. Then I fought it some more.

He wants to expose vulnerability. He wants to bring up some suppressed trauma because there is a rhythm of the womb. Every baby's place in the womb is to be a rocking rhythm. It is a motion and place of security.

Abortion is turbulence and death. Miscarriage is turbulence and death. In the womb, when there are drugs in the baby, there is turbulence and trauma.

Let God Restore You To Wholeness With Nothing Broken & Nothing Missing

The purpose of the womb is a place of safety and the rocking motion that God wants to restore back to you. God wants to restore you to the original condition and the original state.

He wants to restore you to wholeness with nothing broken because He is the prince of peace. Shalom means nothing broken and nothing missing. Staying in His rest and peace will restore you with wholeness.

Let God Set You Free With No Obligations

One day I said to God, "I want to be happy. With all this stuff in ministry, I don't know the way to act. I don't know what to do and then I have this going on and I want to be happy. Ok God! Take out all the obligations! Do everything you are supposed to do and take out of me the obligations! Take out all the 'should have's' and 'could have's!' Take out all the 'I wish I could have!' Take out all the dread of it."

I dreaded the past, dreaded the future, and could not stand the present. We all want the sweet bye and bye and not the "sour now."

Freedom from Seeking For Man's Approval

If you want to be happy, I have many stories to tell. I was obligated to many people in my life and I was afraid of them. Then, God started tearing up all of that.

In particular, He dealt with the ones with whom I sought approval and those whom I was afraid when they were angry. If you grew up with an angry person, it can cause you to be obligated to seek their approval.

I am not saying I was a victim of my childhood. I am saying there were issues. My parents are wonderful people. They are loving parents. Our relationship is being restored to where it should be. We do not work in the ministry together or go to the same church together.

God started to uproot the obligation for approval and suddenly it was gone. All of the ones were gone who I had previously sought for their approval. We want approval from our family and people around us, but Jesus did not get much approval from His family.

Enough Is Enough!!!!

Enough is enough. I had to walk away from the toxic relationships or else they would destroy me. I had to walk away from specific people who were like toxins.

I held onto that word and believed, "Enough is enough. You are done being obligated. You are done!" Being obligated was a scary place to live. I was afraid. That was scary. Fake relationships are pretend and not sincere. They are only surface relationships.

I give Jesus all the glory for what He had done in my life. With God, all things are possible. No matter the circumstance, you are going through, this can be the best day of your life as you change and let go of your past.

Enough is enough when it comes to abuse, control, domination, and stealing your health, joy, peace, and victory in Christ. Don't let the devil steal your heart desires, hope, and ability to succeed in life.

Take time to worship God and get into God's presence. Let Him fill you with peace and joy, restore your identity, and trust in the Lord, for He is good and His mercy endures forever.

This is your new day of transformation to be the whole woman God has called you to be for Him. Let this be a fresh start for change to rise up with your authority in Christ.

See that you a woman of destiny with God's plan, vision, and purpose in your heart and life and you will go forward and never again will you give up.

I pray this book has brought liberty, peace, and joy into your heart and life as you step out of the past, be made whole and transformed by God's love and presence, and take a new step into change and God's destiny for your life!

Chapter 9- Beyond The Great Beyond

About the Author

Beverly D. Kopp pastors alongside of her husband, Pastor Mark C. Kopp, at *"Freedom By The Word Church"* in Wausau, Wisconsin. She is the President of *"Dear Woman Ministries"* and the Director of *"Dear Woman Magazine,"* which was conceived in her heart in November of 1993.

She pioneered the FBTW Bible Training Center, an outreach of her church. She has travelled in missions to minister in Churches and Bible Schools in West Africa, Philippines, and Mexico and ministered in orphanages, and Mission groups in Africa and Russia.

Beverly's goal is to provide the uncompromising Word of God in order to minister life to the whole woman spirit, soul, and body.

Through her "Dear Woman Conferences," literature, magazine, website, outreach ministries, and speaking engagements, she has ministered to hurting, rejected, and abused women of all ages, races, and religions.

It was in 1998 when she stepped out to do the first Dear Woman meeting. She continued with more meetings. She watched as the Holy Spirit ministered to each woman that attended the meetings. The biggest change and healing was in the soul, which included the mind, will, and emotions.

Besides her, many women became free from guilt, shame, envy, rage, and the entire residue from drug and alcohol addiction. The physical healing in her and the other women were amazing. God made the women whole from infertility, tumors, and cancer and healed their backs and bones.

After several years of meetings and conferences, *"Dear Woman"* was put on a shelf. During that time, she and her husband were led into "Special Needs Adoption."

For 6 years, through many classes, seminars and therapy sessions with the six children placed with her and her husband and five additional children for respite, she soon knew it was a direct link to *"Dear Woman Ministries."*

The children they were called to adopt and foster were broken through trauma, abuse, neglect, and rejection. Through the children, they began to understand brokenness and deeper healing took place. They were blessed with two daughters, so far.

At the end of the six years, she proceeded with *"Dear Woman Ministries"* to bring wholeness to hurting, rejected, and abused women. In her conferences and speaking engagements, many women were healed, restored, and made whole.

"Dear Woman Ministries" is now on a new journey. God is taking her ministry north, south, east and west.

*For Prayer or Speaking
Engagement, Contact*

Dear Woman Ministries
Beverly D. Kopp
Website: www.dearwomanministries.org
Email: lk418@msn.com

*For Information or
More Books, Contact*

Freedom By The Word Church
820 S. 8th Ave
Wausau, Wisconsin 54402
Website: www.fbtwc.com